DANA CARLSON

Mindfulness for Kids with Sensory Issues

Building Self-Regulation and Resilience with Mindfulness Strategies

This book was professionally typeset on Reedsy.
Find out more at reedsy.com

Contents

Introduction

Welcome to "Mindfulness for Kids with Sensory Issues." This book is a guide for parents, caregivers, educators, and therapists who are looking to support children with sensory processing challenges through the practice of mindfulness. Sensory issues can profoundly impact a child's daily life, affecting their ability to regulate emotions, engage in social interactions, and participate in everyday activities. However, by integrating mindfulness techniques into their lives, children with sensory sensitivities can develop valuable coping skills and find greater ease in navigating the world around them.

In this book, we will explore the intersection of mindfulness and sensory processing, offering practical strategies and exercises tailored specifically for children with sensory issues. From understanding the fundamentals of sensory processing disorders to introducing mindfulness practices that promote self-awareness and emotional regulation, each chapter is designed to empower both children and caregivers on their journey toward holistic well-being.

Throughout these pages, you will discover a wealth of mindfulness activities and techniques aimed at addressing various aspects of sensory challenges, from managing sensory overload to fostering social connections and enhancing sleep quality.

Additionally, we will delve into the role of mindfulness in supporting sensory integration, self-expression, and resilience in the face of obstacles.

As you embark on this mindfulness journey, remember that progress is a gradual and individualized process. Each child is unique, and their experiences with sensory issues may vary widely. By approaching mindfulness with patience, compassion, and an open mind, we can create a nurturing environment where children feel empowered to explore their sensory experiences mindfully and cultivate a deeper sense of well-being.

Whether you are a parent seeking tools to support your child at home, an educator looking to integrate mindfulness into the classroom, or a therapist guiding children through sensory challenges, this book is here to serve as a valuable resource on your path toward greater understanding, connection, and resilience.

Let's embark on this journey together, embracing mindfulness as a powerful tool for nurturing the holistic well-being of children with sensory issues.

1

Understanding Sensory Issues

1.1 What Are Sensory Issues?

Sensory issues, also known as sensory processing difficulties or sensory processing disorders (SPD), refer to challenges in how the brain processes and responds to sensory stimuli from the environment. These stimuli include sight, sound, touch, taste, smell, and movement. For individuals with sensory issues, these everyday sensations may be experienced more intensely or less intensely than usual, leading to various reactions and behaviors.

One common misconception is that sensory issues only affect one sense or another. However, sensory processing involves the integration of multiple senses, and difficulties can manifest in different ways. For example, a child may be hypersensitive to certain textures, sounds, or smells while being hyposensitive to others. This variability makes sensory issues unique to each individual, requiring personalized approaches to support.

The symptoms of sensory issues can manifest across various domains, including social interactions, emotional regulation, attention, and motor skills. Children with sensory issues may exhibit behaviors such as avoidance of certain stimuli, sensory seeking behaviors (such as spinning or jumping), difficulty with transitions, meltdowns or tantrums in response to sensory overload, and challenges with self-regulation.

1.2 Types of Sensory Processing Disorders

There are three primary patterns of sensory processing disorders:

1. Sensory Modulation Disorder: This type involves difficulties in regulating responses to sensory stimuli. Children with sensory modulation disorder may overreact or underreact to sensory input, leading to challenges in maintaining an optimal level of arousal. This can impact attention, emotional regulation, and behavior.

2. Sensory Discrimination Disorder: Sensory discrimination disorder affects the ability to interpret and differentiate between sensory stimuli accurately. Children with this type of disorder may struggle to distinguish between similar sensations, such as textures or sounds, which can impact their ability to make sense of the world around them.

3. Sensory-Based Motor Disorder: This type involves challenges in coordinating motor movements in response to sensory input. Children with sensory-based motor disorder may have difficulties with balance, coordination, and fine or gross motor skills due to sensory processing deficits.

It's important to note that sensory processing disorders can co-exist with other neurodevelopmental conditions such as autism spectrum disorder, attention-deficit/hyperactivity disorder

(ADHD), and anxiety disorders. Identifying and addressing sensory issues early on can significantly improve the overall well-being and functioning of children.

1.3 Impact of Sensory Issues on Daily Life

The impact of sensory issues on daily life can be profound and far-reaching, affecting various aspects of a child's functioning and development:

- Social Interactions: Sensory issues can influence how children engage with others in social settings. For example, a child who is sensitive to noise may avoid crowded environments or become overwhelmed during group activities. This can lead to social isolation or difficulties in forming friendships.

- Emotional Regulation: Sensory overload or discomfort can trigger emotional responses such as anxiety, frustration, or agitation. Children may have difficulty regulating their emotions in response to sensory stimuli, leading to meltdowns or outbursts.

- Academic Performance: Sensory issues can impact a child's ability to participate and succeed in school. Challenges with sensory processing may interfere with attention, concentration, and learning. For example, a child who is distracted by visual stimuli in the classroom may struggle to focus on academic tasks.

- Daily Activities: Simple daily activities such as dressing, eating, or grooming can become challenging for children with sensory issues. Sensory sensitivities may make certain textures, tastes, or movements aversive, leading to resistance or avoidance of these activities.

- Quality of Life: Overall, sensory issues can significantly impact a child's quality of life and well-being. Persistent sensory discomfort or overload can cause stress and anxiety, affecting sleep, mood, and overall functioning.

Understanding the profound impact of sensory issues on daily life is essential for developing effective strategies and interventions to support children in managing their sensory challenges. By recognizing and addressing sensory needs, we can help children thrive and reach their full potential.

2

Introduction to Mindfulness

Chapter 2 of "Mindfulness for Kids with Sensory Issues" dives into the fundamental aspects of mindfulness, its profound benefits for children, and its particular relevance in addressing sensory issues.

2.1 What is Mindfulness?

Mindfulness, rooted in ancient contemplative traditions such as Buddhism, has gained significant recognition in contemporary psychology and wellness practices. At its core, mindfulness refers to the intentional and non-judgmental awareness of the present moment. It involves observing thoughts, emotions, bodily sensations, and the surrounding environment with openness and acceptance.

Central to mindfulness practice is cultivating a state of focused attention, often anchored by the breath or bodily sensations.

Through mindfulness meditation, individuals learn to acknowledge and let go of distracting thoughts, fostering a sense of clarity and inner calm. The practice encourages a compassionate attitude towards oneself and others, promoting emotional regulation and resilience.

For children, mindfulness can be introduced through age-appropriate activities and exercises tailored to their developmental stage. Simple practices like mindful breathing, body scans, and sensory awareness games help children cultivate attentional skills and emotional awareness. By engaging in mindfulness, children learn to navigate their inner world with curiosity and kindness, laying the foundation for lifelong well-being.

2.2 Benefits of Mindfulness for Children

The benefits of mindfulness for children are multifaceted and extend across various domains of development. Research has shown that regular mindfulness practice can enhance cognitive abilities, emotional regulation, and social skills in children.

One significant advantage of mindfulness is its positive impact on attentional control. Through practices like focused breathing or mindful listening, children learn to sustain their attention on the present moment, improving their ability to concentrate and stay focused in academic and social settings. This enhanced attentional capacity also translates into better academic performance and problem-solving skills.

Moreover, mindfulness fosters emotional intelligence by promoting self-awareness and self-regulation. By tuning into their thoughts and feelings without judgment, children develop a deeper understanding of their inner experiences and learn to manage challenging emotions effectively. Mindfulness practices teach children to respond to stressful situations with equanimity, reducing impulsivity and aggression while promoting empathy and compassion towards others.

In addition to cognitive and emotional benefits, mindfulness nurtures resilience and mental well-being in children. By cultivating a non-reactive stance towards life's ups and downs, children learn to bounce back from setbacks and adversity with greater ease. Mindfulness practices provide children with valuable coping strategies for managing stress, anxiety, and overwhelming sensory experiences. As a result, they develop a more balanced and resilient mindset, empowering them to navigate life's challenges with confidence and courage.

2.3 How Mindfulness Can Help with Sensory Issues

Sensory issues, commonly associated with conditions like autism spectrum disorder (ASD) and sensory processing disorder (SPD), can significantly impact a child's daily functioning and quality of life. Sensory sensitivity or sensory seeking behaviors may manifest as heightened reactivity to sensory stimuli, such as loud noises, bright lights, or certain textures, leading to sensory overload or avoidance behaviors.

Mindfulness offers a promising approach for supporting children with sensory issues by helping them regulate their sensory experiences and cultivate greater awareness of their bodily sensations. Through mindfulness practices, children learn to tune into their sensory experiences with curiosity and acceptance, rather than reacting with fear or aversion.

For children with sensory sensitivities, mindfulness can serve as a powerful tool for self-regulation. By practicing mindful breathing or body scans, children develop a greater awareness of their bodily responses to sensory stimuli, allowing them to recognize early signs of sensory overload and implement coping strategies proactively. Mindfulness teaches children to ground themselves in the present moment, providing a sense of stability and safety amidst sensory challenges.

Moreover, mindfulness encourages a non-judgmental attitude towards sensory experiences, helping children reframe their perceptions of discomfort or overwhelm. By cultivating a mindset of acceptance and curiosity, children learn to approach sensory stimuli with openness and resilience, rather than avoidance or resistance. This shift in perspective empowers children to engage more fully in their environment and participate in activities they may have previously avoided due to sensory discomfort.

Furthermore, mindfulness practices promote emotional regulation skills that are essential for managing sensory issues effectively. By learning to observe their thoughts and feelings without judgment, children develop greater self-awareness and emotional resilience, enabling them to cope with sensory triggers more adaptively. Mindfulness teaches children to respond to sensory challenges with calmness and equanimity, reducing the likelihood of meltdowns or emotional dysregulation.

In summary, Chapter 2 provides an in-depth exploration of mindfulness, its myriad benefits for children, and its transformative potential in addressing sensory issues. By introducing children to mindfulness practices early in life, we equip them with invaluable tools for cultivating attention, emotional resilience, and sensory regulation, empowering them to thrive in an increasingly complex world.

3

Getting Started with Mindfulness Practices

Chapter 3 explains the foundational aspects of introducing mindfulness practices to children with sensory issues. Through a structured approach, this chapter aims to create a safe and welcoming environment conducive to mindfulness exploration. It begins with the establishment of a secure space, progresses to the fundamental technique of mindful breathing, and culminates in the exploration of body scan techniques.

3.1 Creating a Safe Space for Mindfulness

Creating a safe space for mindfulness is essential, especially for children with sensory sensitivities. This space serves as a sanctuary where children can feel comfortable and at ease, allowing them to fully engage in mindfulness practices without distractions or discomfort.

To create such a space, consider the physical environment. Choose a quiet, clutter-free area with soft lighting and comfortable seating. Removing potential sensory triggers, such as loud noises or harsh lighting, can help children feel more relaxed and focused during their mindfulness practice.

In addition to the physical environment, it's crucial to cultivate a supportive atmosphere. Encourage open communication and empathy among participants. Validate children's experiences and emotions, reassuring them that it's okay to feel whatever arises during mindfulness practice.

Moreover, incorporate sensory elements into the space to engage multiple senses. Soft blankets or cushions can provide tactile comfort, while soothing music or nature sounds can create a calming auditory backdrop. Consider adding elements of nature, such as plants or natural materials, to promote a sense of connection and grounding.

Ultimately, the goal is to create a safe and inviting space where children feel empowered to explore mindfulness at their own pace, free from judgment or pressure.

3.2 Introduction to Mindful Breathing

Mindful breathing is a foundational mindfulness technique that involves focusing one's attention on the breath as it flows in and out of the body. This simple yet powerful practice can help children develop awareness of their breath, regulate their emotions, and cultivate a sense of calm.

To introduce mindful breathing to children, start by explaining the concept in simple terms. Emphasize that mindful breathing involves paying attention to the breath without trying to change it. Encourage children to find a comfortable position, whether sitting or lying down, and invite them to close their eyes if they feel comfortable doing so.

Next, guide children through a brief mindful breathing exercise. Encourage them to notice the sensation of the breath as it enters and leaves the body. They can focus on the rising and falling of their chest or the feeling of air passing through their nostrils. Remind children that it's normal for the mind to wander, and gently encourage them to bring their attention back to the breath whenever they notice distraction.

As children become more familiar with mindful breathing, they can experiment with different variations, such as counting breaths or pairing the breath with affirmations or visualizations. Encourage them to practice mindful breathing regularly, both during formal meditation sessions and in everyday life whenever they need a moment of calm or grounding.

3.3 Exploring Body Scan Techniques

The body scan is a mindfulness practice that involves systematically bringing awareness to different parts of the body, from head to toe. This technique can help children develop greater body awareness, release tension, and cultivate a sense of relaxation.

To introduce body scan techniques to children, begin by explaining the concept in simple terms. Let them know that they will be focusing their attention on different parts of their body, one at a time, and noticing any sensations they experience without judgment.

Guide children through a body scan exercise by instructing them to start at the top of their head and gradually move down through their body, paying attention to each area in turn. Encourage them to notice any sensations they experience, such as warmth, tingling, or tension, without trying to change them.

As children become more comfortable with the body scan, they can experiment with different variations, such as focusing on specific sensations or incorporating deep breathing into the practice. Encourage them to practice the body scan regularly, either as a standalone exercise or as part of a longer mindfulness session.

By introducing children to the practice of mindful breathing and body scan techniques in a safe and supportive environment, Chapter 3 lays the groundwork for their mindfulness journey. These foundational practices provide children with valuable tools for developing self-awareness, managing stress, and cultivating a greater sense of well-being in their daily lives.

4

Mindfulness Activities for Sensory Regulation

Sensory regulation is crucial for individuals with sensory processing disorders as it helps them manage their responses to sensory stimuli in their environment effectively. In this chapter, we explore three key techniques: Grounding Techniques for Overwhelm, Sensory-Focused Mindful Movement, and Using Mindfulness to Manage Sensory Overload.

4.1 Grounding Techniques for Overwhelm

When children experience sensory overload or overwhelming sensations, grounding techniques can provide a sense of stability and calmness. Grounding techniques aim to anchor the individual to the present moment, helping them feel more centered and in control. Here are some steps to implement grounding techniques:

Step 1: Awareness - Encourage the child to recognize the signs of overwhelm or sensory overload. This could include increased heart rate, shallow breathing, or heightened agitation.

Step 2: Pause and Breathe - Guide the child to pause whatever they are doing and take slow, deep breaths. Breathing deeply activates the parasympathetic nervous system, promoting relaxation and reducing stress.

Step 3: Name Sensations - Prompt the child to identify and name the sensations they are experiencing. This could include physical sensations such as tension in the body or emotional sensations like anxiety or fear.

Step 4: Engage the Senses - Encourage the child to engage their senses to bring their attention back to the present moment. This could involve touching different textures, listening to calming music, or focusing on the sights and sounds around them.

Step 5: Grounding Objects - Provide the child with grounding objects such as a stress ball, a favorite toy, or a smooth stone to hold onto. These objects can serve as anchors, helping the child feel more grounded and secure.

Step 6: Affirmations - Introduce affirmations or positive statements that the child can repeat to themselves to reinforce feelings of safety and calmness. For example, "I am safe," "I am in control," or "This feeling will pass."

Step 7: Reflect and Review - After the grounding exercise, take a moment to reflect on the experience with the child. Ask them how they feel now compared to before the exercise and encourage them to use these techniques whenever they feel overwhelmed in the future.

4.2 Sensory-Focused Mindful Movement

Mindful movement involves engaging in physical activities with deliberate attention and awareness, incorporating sensory input to regulate the nervous system. Here's how to incorporate sensory-focused mindful movement:

Step 1: Choose Activities - Select activities that provide sensory input and promote body awareness, such as yoga, tai chi, or sensory walks.

Step 2: Mindful Warm-Up - Begin with a mindful warm-up to connect the child with their body and breath. This could include gentle stretching, deep breathing exercises, or body scan meditation.

Step 3: Sensory Exploration - Encourage the child to explore different sensory experiences while moving their body. This could involve feeling the texture of the ground beneath their feet, noticing the sensation of air on their skin, or listening to the sounds of nature.

Step 4: Slow and Controlled Movements - Guide the child to move slowly and deliberately, paying attention to the sensations in their body with each movement. Emphasize the importance of staying present and focused on the experience.

Step 5: Breath Awareness - Remind the child to synchronize their movements with their breath, inhaling as they expand or lengthen and exhaling as they contract or release tension.

Step 6: Mindful Resting - Incorporate periods of mindful resting between movements to allow the child to observe any changes in their body and sensations.

Step 7: Reflective Practice - After the mindful movement activity, facilitate a reflective practice where the child can share their experience and any insights gained from the practice.

4.3 Using Mindfulness to Manage Sensory Overload

Mindfulness techniques can be powerful tools for managing sensory overload by helping individuals regulate their responses to overwhelming stimuli. Here's how to use mindfulness to manage sensory overload:

Step 1: Awareness of Triggers - Help the child identify specific triggers that contribute to sensory overload. This could include loud noises, bright lights, crowded spaces, or certain textures.

Step 2: Mindful Observation - Encourage the child to observe their thoughts, emotions, and physical sensations when they encounter sensory triggers. Teach them to notice without judgment and acknowledge the experience with curiosity and openness.

Step 3: Grounding Techniques - Introduce grounding techniques, such as deep breathing, sensory exploration, or grounding objects, to help the child cope with sensory overload in the moment.

Step 4: Mindful Distraction – Teach the child to use mindfulness as a form of distraction from overwhelming stimuli. This could involve focusing on their breath, engaging in a sensory activity, or visualizing a calming place.

Step 5: Relaxation Techniques – Guide the child through relaxation techniques such as progressive muscle relaxation, guided imagery, or body scan meditation to reduce physiological arousal and promote relaxation.

Step 6: Coping Strategies – Collaborate with the child to develop personalized coping strategies for managing sensory overload in different situations. Encourage them to experiment with different techniques and identify what works best for them.

Step 7: Practice and Patience – Remind the child that managing sensory overload is a skill that requires practice and patience. Encourage them to be gentle with themselves and celebrate progress, no matter how small.

In conclusion, Chapter 4 provides a comprehensive guide to mindfulness activities for sensory regulation, including grounding techniques for overwhelm, sensory-focused mindful movement, and using mindfulness to manage sensory overload. By incorporating these techniques into their daily lives, children with sensory issues can develop greater self-awareness, resilience, and emotional regulation skills to navigate their sensory experiences more effectively.

5

Mindfulness and Emotional Regulation

Emotions are an integral part of human experience, shaping our perceptions, decisions, and interactions with the world. For children with sensory issues, navigating emotions can be particularly challenging due to heightened sensory responses and difficulty in regulating reactions. In this chapter, we look into the intersection of mindfulness and emotional regulation, exploring techniques and strategies to help children understand their emotions, manage anger effectively, and cultivate compassion and self-regulation.

5.1 Understanding Emotions and Sensory Responses

Children with sensory issues often experience emotions in a heightened manner, influenced by their sensory sensitivities. For example, a loud noise or overwhelming sensory input may trigger feelings of anxiety or frustration. Understanding these emotions and their sensory triggers is crucial in developing effective emotional regulation strategies.

Mindfulness offers a powerful tool for enhancing emotional awareness. Through mindfulness practices, children learn to observe their emotions without judgment, acknowledging them as passing experiences rather than defining aspects of themselves. Mindfulness encourages children to tune into their bodily sensations, recognizing how emotions manifest physically. By developing this awareness, children can better identify and label their emotions, fostering a deeper understanding of their inner experiences.

To facilitate emotional awareness, mindfulness activities such as body scans and mindful breathing can be particularly beneficial. Body scans involve systematically directing attention to different parts of the body, noticing any sensations or tensions present. This practice encourages children to connect with their bodily experiences, enhancing their ability to recognize and interpret emotional signals.

Moreover, mindful breathing serves as a grounding technique, enabling children to anchor themselves in the present moment amidst emotional turbulence. By focusing on the sensations of each breath—its rise and fall, the expansion and contraction of the chest—children develop resilience in the face of intense emotions, cultivating a sense of calm and stability.

5.2 Mindfulness for Anger Management

Anger is a common emotion experienced by children with sensory issues, often stemming from sensory overload or frustration with environmental stimuli. Without effective coping mechanisms, anger can escalate, leading to meltdowns or disruptive behaviors. Mindfulness offers a proactive approach to anger management, empowering children to respond to anger in a constructive manner.

One key mindfulness practice for anger management is the "STOP" technique. When a child feels anger arising, they are encouraged to pause and take a mindful breath, allowing them to step back from the immediate intensity of the emotion. Next, they observe their thoughts and bodily sensations without reacting impulsively. This step involves acknowledging the anger without fueling it further through rumination or resistance. Then, the child proceeds to widen their perspective, considering alternative responses and the potential consequences of their actions. Finally, they choose how to respond mindfully, selecting a course of action aligned with their values and well-being.

In addition to the "STOP" technique, mindfulness-based interventions such as loving-kindness meditation can foster compassion and empathy towards oneself and others. By cultivating a sense of goodwill and understanding, children learn to approach situations with kindness rather than aggression, diffusing conflicts and promoting harmonious relationships.

5.3 Cultivating Compassion and Self-Regulation

Compassion towards oneself and others is a fundamental aspect of emotional regulation, nurturing resilience and fostering positive social connections. For children with sensory issues, who may face challenges in self-regulation, cultivating compassion through mindfulness practices is particularly valuable.

A cornerstone of compassion-focused mindfulness is self-compassion, which involves treating oneself with kindness and understanding, especially in moments of difficulty or distress. Mindfulness exercises such as the "self-compassion break" guide children to acknowledge their struggles with gentleness and acceptance, recognizing that suffering is a universal human experience. By offering themselves words of comfort and reassurance, children develop inner resources to navigate emotional upheavals with greater resilience.

Moreover, mindfulness practices can enhance self-regulation by strengthening executive functions such as impulse control and cognitive flexibility. Through regular practice, children develop greater awareness of their thoughts and emotions, allowing them to regulate their responses consciously rather than reacting impulsively. Techniques such as mindful breathing and visualization empower children to pause and recalibrate their emotional state, fostering emotional balance and self-control.

In conclusion, mindfulness offers a holistic approach to emotional regulation for children with sensory issues, integrating awareness, compassion, and self-regulation. By cultivating mindfulness, children develop the tools and resilience to navigate their emotions skillfully, fostering greater well-being and adaptive functioning in daily life.

6

Mindfulness and Social Interactions

For children with sensory sensitivities, navigating social situations can be overwhelming and challenging. This chapter aims to provide a comprehensive guide on how mindfulness practices can help children develop essential social skills, such as mindful listening, effective communication, and building empathy in relationships.

6.1 Navigating Social Situations with Sensory Sensitivities

Children with sensory sensitivities often find social situations overwhelming due to the sensory stimuli they encounter. Loud noises, bright lights, crowded spaces, and unexpected touch can trigger feelings of anxiety and discomfort. Mindfulness offers valuable tools to help children navigate these situations more effectively.

Firstly, mindfulness teaches children to recognize their sensory experiences without judgment. Through practices such as mindful breathing and body scans, children learn to observe their thoughts, emotions, and physical sensations as they arise in social settings. By acknowledging these experiences without reacting impulsively, children can cultivate a greater sense of self-awareness and emotional regulation.

Moreover, mindfulness encourages children to develop coping strategies for managing sensory overload. Techniques such as grounding exercises and sensory-focused mindfulness activities provide children with practical tools to ground themselves in the present moment and regulate their sensory experiences. For example, a child experiencing sensory overwhelm in a noisy environment can practice mindful breathing to anchor themselves and reduce feelings of anxiety.

Additionally, mindfulness helps children cultivate resilience in the face of social challenges. By fostering a nonjudgmental attitude towards themselves and others, children can approach social interactions with greater openness and curiosity. Mindfulness teaches children to respond to social situations with kindness and compassion, even when faced with adversity or misunderstanding.

Overall, mindfulness empowers children with sensory sensitivities to navigate social situations with greater confidence, resilience, and self-awareness.

6.2 Mindful Listening and Communication Skills

Effective communication is essential for building meaningful relationships and navigating social interactions successfully. Mindful listening and communication skills play a crucial role in helping children with sensory sensitivities connect with others and express themselves more effectively.

Mindful listening involves fully attending to and understanding what others are saying without judgment or distraction. For children with sensory sensitivities, practicing mindful listening can be particularly beneficial as it helps them focus their attention on the speaker's words rather than becoming overwhelmed by sensory stimuli in the environment.

One mindfulness technique that supports mindful listening is "mindful speaking and listening circles." In this practice, children take turns speaking while others listen mindfully without interrupting or judging. This promotes active listening skills and encourages children to express themselves authentically while feeling heard and valued by others.

Additionally, mindfulness enhances communication skills by teaching children to communicate with clarity, empathy, and respect. Through practices such as loving-kindness meditation and compassionate communication exercises, children learn to communicate their thoughts and feelings honestly while considering the perspectives and emotions of others.

Moreover, mindfulness fosters emotional awareness and regulation, which are essential components of effective communication. By becoming more attuned to their own emotions and those of others, children can express themselves more authentically and respond to social cues with greater sensitivity and empathy.

Overall, mindful listening and communication skills are vital for helping children with sensory sensitivities build positive relationships, express themselves confidently, and navigate social interactions with greater ease and understanding.

6.3 Building Empathy and Understanding in Relationships

Empathy is the ability to understand and share the feelings of others, and it forms the foundation of healthy relationships. For children with sensory sensitivities, developing empathy can be challenging due to difficulties in understanding and interpreting social cues. However, mindfulness practices can help children cultivate empathy and understanding in their relationships.

Mindfulness encourages children to develop a deeper awareness of their own emotions and experiences, which lays the groundwork for empathy towards others. By practicing self-compassion and loving-kindness meditation, children learn to extend kindness and understanding to themselves, which naturally extends to others.

Furthermore, mindfulness fosters perspective-taking skills by encouraging children to consider different viewpoints and experiences. Through practices such as "seeing through the eyes of others," children learn to empathize with the thoughts, feelings, and experiences of their peers, even if they may not fully understand or relate to them.

Additionally, mindfulness promotes active listening and attunement to the emotions of others, which are essential components of empathy. By tuning into the nonverbal cues and subtle signals of their peers, children can better understand their feelings and respond with empathy and compassion.

Moreover, mindfulness practices can help children develop healthy boundaries and assertive communication skills, which are essential for maintaining positive relationships. By learning to assert their own needs and preferences while respecting those of others, children can navigate social interactions more effectively and build deeper connections with their peers.

Overall, mindfulness plays a crucial role in helping children with sensory sensitivities develop empathy, understanding, and healthy relationships with others. By cultivating mindfulness in their daily lives, children can navigate social interactions with greater compassion, empathy, and respect for themselves and others.

7

Mindfulness in Everyday Activities

Mindfulness in everyday activities is about bringing focused awareness and presence to the tasks we do regularly, transforming them into opportunities for self-awareness, relaxation, and growth. In this chapter, we explore how mindfulness can be integrated into various daily routines, including eating habits, school and learning environments, and overall daily activities.

7.1 Applying Mindfulness to Eating Habits

Eating is not just a biological necessity but also a sensory experience that can be enriched through mindfulness. Mindful eating involves paying full attention to the sensory experience of eating, including the taste, texture, smell, and even the sounds of the food. Here are some steps to apply mindfulness to eating habits:

1. Preparation: Before eating, take a moment to appreciate the

food in front of you. Notice the colors, textures, and smells. This helps to engage the senses and prepare the mind for mindful eating.

2. Setting the Environment: Create a calm and peaceful environment for eating, free from distractions like television or electronic devices. Sit down at a table and take a few deep breaths to center yourself.

3. Mindful Eating: As you begin to eat, take small bites and chew slowly. Pay attention to the taste and texture of the food as you chew. Notice the sensations of swallowing and the feeling of fullness or satisfaction.

4. Pause Between Bites: After each bite, put down your utensils and take a moment to check in with your body. Are you still hungry? How does the food make you feel? This helps to prevent mindless overeating and allows you to honor your body's signals of hunger and fullness.

5. Gratitude: Cultivate a sense of gratitude for the food you are eating and the nourishment it provides to your body. Reflect on the effort that went into producing the food, from planting and harvesting to cooking and serving.

By practicing mindful eating, you can develop a healthier relationship with food, reduce overeating, and enhance your overall well-being.

7.2 Mindfulness in School and Learning Environments

School and learning environments can be stressful and over-whelming for children, especially those with sensory issues. Mindfulness techniques can help students cultivate focus, man-age stress, and enhance their learning experience. Here's how mindfulness can be incorporated into school settings:

1. Mindful Breathing: Begin each class or learning session with a brief mindfulness exercise, such as mindful breathing. Invite students to close their eyes and focus on their breath for a few moments, bringing their attention to the present moment and letting go of any distractions or worries.

2. Mindful Movement: Incorporate brief movement breaks throughout the day to help students release tension and regain focus. Simple yoga poses or stretching exercises can be practiced mindfully, with an emphasis on connecting movement with breath and awareness.

3. Mindful Listening: Teach students the importance of mindful listening during class discussions or group activities. Encourage them to listen attentively to their peers without judgment or interruption, fostering empathy and understanding in the classroom.

4. Mindful Study Habits: Encourage students to approach studying and homework with mindfulness. Suggest techniques such as setting aside dedicated study time, breaking tasks into smaller manageable chunks, and taking regular breaks to rest and recharge.

5. Mindful Reflection: At the end of each day or week, provide op-

portunities for students to reflect on their learning experiences. Ask open-ended questions that encourage self-awareness and introspection, such as "What did you learn today?" or "How did you overcome challenges?"

By integrating mindfulness into school and learning environments, educators can support students in developing essential life skills such as attention regulation, emotional resilience, and self-awareness.

7.3 Incorporating Mindfulness into Daily Routines

Incorporating mindfulness into daily routines is essential for maintaining a consistent mindfulness practice and reaping its benefits in everyday life. Here are some ways to incorporate mindfulness into daily routines:

1. Morning Routine: Start your day with a mindfulness practice, such as meditation or mindful movement. Set aside a few minutes each morning to center yourself and set positive intentions for the day ahead.

2. Commute: Use your commute time as an opportunity for mindfulness. Whether you're walking, driving, or taking public transportation, bring awareness to your surroundings and the sensations in your body.

3. Work or School: Take regular breaks throughout the day to practice mindfulness. This could be as simple as taking a few deep breaths, stretching at your desk, or practicing mindful eating during lunchtime.

4. Evening Routine: Wind down at the end of the day with a calming mindfulness practice, such as a body scan or gentle yoga. Reflect on the events of the day with gratitude and compassion, letting go of any stress or tension.

5. Bedtime Ritual: Establish a bedtime ritual that promotes relaxation and restful sleep. This could include activities such as reading, journaling, or practicing a guided meditation for sleep.

By incorporating mindfulness into daily routines, you can cultivate a greater sense of presence, resilience, and well-being in your life.

In conclusion, mindfulness can be integrated into various aspects of daily life, from eating habits and school environments to overall daily routines. By practicing mindfulness in these activities, children with sensory issues can develop essential life skills such as self-awareness, emotional regulation, and stress management, ultimately leading to improved well-being and quality of life.

8

Mindfulness and Sleep

Sleep is a vital component of overall well-being, yet for children with sensory issues, achieving restful sleep can be a considerable challenge. In this chapter, we look into understanding the unique sleep challenges faced by individuals with sensory issues, explore mindfulness techniques tailored to improve sleep quality, and discuss the creation of a bedtime mindfulness ritual to promote relaxation and restfulness.

8.1 Understanding Sleep Challenges with Sensory Issues

Individuals with sensory issues often experience heightened sensitivity to various stimuli, which can significantly impact their ability to fall asleep and maintain restful sleep throughout the night. Common sensory challenges include sensitivity to light, sound, touch, and environmental factors such as temperature and texture.

For children with sensory processing disorders, bedtime routines may trigger anxiety and overstimulation rather than relaxation. Bright lights, loud noises, uncomfortable bedding, or irregular sleep schedules can disrupt their natural sleep patterns, leading to sleep disturbances and fatigue during the day.

Furthermore, sensory issues may exacerbate other sleep-related conditions such as insomnia, sleep apnea, or restless leg syndrome, further complicating the sleep landscape for these individuals. It's crucial for parents and caregivers to recognize the interplay between sensory issues and sleep disturbances to develop targeted interventions that address the root causes of sleep disruptions.

8.2 Mindfulness Techniques for Better Sleep

Mindfulness practices offer valuable tools for individuals with sensory issues to cultivate a sense of calm, reduce anxiety, and promote relaxation, all of which are essential for improving sleep quality. Here are several mindfulness techniques specifically tailored to address sleep challenges:

- Deep Breathing Exercises: Encourage deep diaphragmatic breathing to activate the body's relaxation response and calm the nervous system. Teach children to focus on the sensation of their breath as it enters and exits their body, allowing them to anchor their attention in the present moment and let go of racing thoughts or worries.

- Progressive Muscle Relaxation: Guide children through a

series of muscle relaxation exercises, systematically tensing and releasing different muscle groups throughout the body. This technique promotes physical relaxation, relieves tension, and prepares the body for sleep.

- Body Scan Meditation: Lead children through a body scan meditation, where they gently direct their attention to each part of their body, noticing any sensations without judgment or attachment. By cultivating body awareness, children can release tension and promote a sense of ease and comfort conducive to sleep.

- Visualizations and Guided Imagery: Use guided imagery scripts or visualization exercises to create calming mental images that evoke feelings of safety, security, and tranquility. Encourage children to imagine themselves in a peaceful setting, such as a serene beach or a quiet forest, allowing them to escape from stressors and unwind before bedtime.

- Sensory-Based Relaxation Techniques: Incorporate sensory-based mindfulness practices, such as aromatherapy, gentle touch, or weighted blankets, to soothe the nervous system and create a sensory-friendly sleep environment. Experiment with different sensory modalities to identify which techniques resonate most with each individual's preferences and needs.

8.3 Creating a Bedtime Mindfulness Ritual

Establishing a consistent bedtime routine infused with mindfulness practices can signal to the body and mind that it's time to unwind and prepare for sleep. A bedtime mindfulness ritual can help children with sensory issues transition from the busyness of the day to a state of relaxation and restfulness. Here's how to create an effective bedtime mindfulness ritual:

- Set the Stage: Create a calm and soothing sleep environment free from distractions and sensory triggers. Dim the lights, adjust the room temperature, and remove any electronic devices or stimulating activities that may interfere with relaxation.

- Mindful Preparation: Encourage children to engage in relaxing activities leading up to bedtime, such as reading a book, taking a warm bath, or practicing gentle yoga stretches. These activities help shift their focus away from stressors and promote a sense of ease and tranquility.

- Mindful Breathing: Incorporate deep breathing exercises into the bedtime routine to promote relaxation and centering. Guide children to take slow, deep breaths, counting the inhale and exhale to establish a rhythm that calms the nervous system.

- Sensory Comfort: Provide sensory-friendly bedding, pajamas, and sleep accessories that cater to each child's individual sensory preferences. Weighted blankets, soft textures, and calming scents can enhance comfort and promote a sense of security during sleep.

- Guided Relaxation: Lead children through a guided relaxation or visualization exercise to help them unwind and release tension from their bodies and minds. Use soothing language and gentle imagery to create a peaceful mental landscape conducive to sleep.

- Reflection and Gratitude: Encourage children to reflect on positive experiences from their day and cultivate a sense of gratitude before drifting off to sleep. This practice fosters a positive mindset and promotes feelings of contentment and well-being.

By incorporating mindfulness techniques into a bedtime ritual, children with sensory issues can develop healthy sleep habits and experience more restful and rejuvenating sleep. Consistency and patience are keys as children adjust to their new bedtime routine and reap the benefits of mindfulness for improved sleep quality and overall well-being.

9

Mindfulness and Sensory Integration

This chapter focuses on the crucial intersection between mindfulness and sensory integration, offering insights into how mindfulness practices can complement sensory integration therapy and occupational therapy techniques to support children with sensory issues. Sensory integration refers to the brain's ability to organize and interpret sensory information from the environment to produce an appropriate response. For children with sensory processing disorders, this process can be challenging, leading to difficulties in regulating emotions, behavior, and participation in daily activities. By integrating mindfulness into sensory integration therapy and occupational therapy, practitioners and caregivers can enhance the effectiveness of interventions and promote holistic well-being.

9.1 Exploring Sensory Integration Therapy

Sensory integration therapy is a specialized approach designed to help individuals process and respond to sensory information more effectively. It aims to improve sensory processing abilities through structured activities that provide sensory input in a controlled environment. Central to sensory integration therapy is the concept of adaptive responses, where individuals learn to modulate their responses to sensory stimuli in a way that supports participation in meaningful activities.

Key components of sensory integration therapy include:

- Sensory assessment: Before initiating therapy, a comprehensive sensory assessment is conducted to identify the individual's sensory preferences, sensitivities, and challenges. This assessment helps therapists tailor interventions to meet the unique needs of each child.

- Sensory diet: Based on the assessment findings, therapists develop a personalized "sensory diet" consisting of activities designed to provide the individual with the sensory input they need to regulate their arousal levels and enhance attention and engagement. These activities may include tactile, proprioceptive, vestibular, auditory, and visual experiences.

- Sensory-rich environment: Therapy sessions take place in a sensory-rich environment equipped with various equipment and materials to facilitate sensory exploration and integration. Swings, trampolines, tactile bins, and balance boards are examples of tools used to provide sensory input and promote adaptive responses.

- Therapeutic activities: Therapists guide individuals through a range of therapeutic activities aimed at improving sensory processing skills, motor coordination, and self-regulation. These activities may involve sensory-motor challenges, balance activities, fine motor tasks, and social interactions in a supportive environment.

- Gradual progression: Therapy sessions are structured to gradually increase the complexity and intensity of sensory experiences, allowing individuals to build tolerance and adaptability over time. Therapists monitor progress closely and adjust interventions as needed to support continued growth and development.

By incorporating mindfulness principles into sensory integration therapy, practitioners can enhance the effectiveness of interventions by promoting present-moment awareness, self-regulation, and emotional resilience. Mindfulness encourages individuals to observe their sensory experiences without judgment, allowing them to develop a greater sense of control and acceptance.

9.2 Mindfulness Practices to Support Sensory Integration

Mindfulness practices offer a valuable complement to sensory integration therapy by promoting self-awareness, relaxation, and adaptive coping strategies. These practices cultivate a mindful approach to sensory experiences, enabling individuals to respond to stimuli with greater ease and flexibility. Here are some mindfulness techniques that can support sensory integration:

- Mindful breathing: Encourage children to focus on their breath as a way to anchor their attention and regulate their arousal levels. Deep breathing exercises can help calm the nervous system and promote relaxation, making it easier to engage in sensory activities.

- Body scan: Guide children through a body scan meditation, where they systematically bring awareness to each part of their body, noticing any sensations without judgment. This practice promotes body awareness and helps individuals identify areas of tension or discomfort that may impact sensory processing.

- Sensory mindfulness: Encourage children to approach sensory experiences with curiosity and openness, using their senses to explore the present moment fully. Whether it's feeling the texture of an object, listening to sounds in the environment, or noticing the colors and shapes around them, sensory mindfulness fosters a deeper connection to the world.

- Grounding techniques: Teach children grounding techniques such as mindfulness of the breath, visualization, or progressive muscle relaxation to help them feel more anchored and present in their bodies. These techniques can be particularly beneficial during times of sensory overload or emotional distress.

- Mindful movement: Incorporate mindful movement activities such as yoga, tai chi, or dance into therapy sessions to promote body awareness, coordination, and balance. Mindful movement practices encourage individuals to move with intention and grace, fostering a sense of embodied mindfulness.

By integrating mindfulness practices into sensory integration therapy, therapists can empower children to develop greater self-awareness, resilience, and adaptive coping skills in the face of sensory challenges.

9.3 Integrating Mindfulness into Occupational Therapy

Occupational therapists play a vital role in supporting children with sensory issues to participate in meaningful activities and develop essential life skills. By integrating mindfulness into occupational therapy interventions, therapists can enhance the effectiveness of treatment plans and promote holistic well-being. Here are some ways mindfulness can be integrated into occupational therapy:

- Mindful goal setting: Begin therapy sessions with a mindful check-in to help children connect with their feelings, thoughts, and goals for the session. Encourage them to set intentions for their therapy work, focusing on areas they want to explore or improve.

- Mindful self-regulation: Teach children mindfulness techniques such as deep breathing, progressive muscle relaxation, or guided imagery to help them regulate their emotions and arousal levels. These techniques can be used as part of a sensory diet or as coping strategies during challenging situations.

- Mindful engagement in activities: Encourage children to approach occupational therapy activities with mindfulness, paying attention to their sensations, thoughts, and emotions as they participate. Whether it's completing a puzzle, writing in a journal, or engaging in sensory play, mindfulness can enhance the therapeutic benefits of these activities.

- Mindful transitions: Help children transition mindfully between activities or environments by providing prompts or cues to bring awareness to the present moment. This can help reduce anxiety and increase engagement in therapy sessions.

- Mindful reflection: Incorporate reflective practices into therapy sessions to help children process their experiences and insights. Invite them to share their thoughts and feelings about their progress, challenges, and successes, fostering a sense of self-awareness and agency.

By integrating mindfulness into occupational therapy, therapists can empower children to develop essential skills for navigating daily life with greater ease and confidence. Mindfulness-based approaches enhance self-awareness, emotional regulation, and adaptive coping strategies, promoting holistic well-being and resilience in children with sensory issues.

In conclusion, Chapter 9 explores the synergistic relationship between mindfulness and sensory integration, highlighting how mindfulness practices can enhance the effectiveness of sensory integration therapy and occupational therapy interventions for children with sensory issues. By integrating mindfulness into therapeutic approaches, practitioners and caregivers can support children in developing essential skills for self-regulation, emotional resilience, and participation in meaningful activities. Through mindfulness, children can cultivate a deeper connection to their sensory experiences and develop adaptive coping strategies to navigate the complexities of the world around them.

10

Mindfulness and Self-Expression

Mindfulness and self-expression are intricately intertwined, offering children with sensory issues a powerful avenue for exploring their creativity and inner worlds. In this chapter, we delve into various mindful practices that facilitate self-expression, including using mindfulness to explore creativity, engaging in art therapy, and incorporating writing and journaling into daily routines.

10.1 Using Mindfulness to Explore Creativity

Mindfulness serves as a gateway to unlocking creativity by encouraging children to engage fully in the present moment without judgment. Through mindfulness practices, children can cultivate a deeper awareness of their thoughts, emotions, and sensations, fostering a fertile ground for creative expression.

To begin using mindfulness to explore creativity, children

can start with simple mindfulness exercises such as mindful breathing or body scan meditation. These practices help them become more attuned to their inner experiences, allowing creative ideas to flow more freely.

Next, encourage children to engage in activities that stimulate their senses and ignite their imagination. This could involve sensory exploration through nature walks, art projects, or music appreciation. By fully immersing themselves in sensory experiences with mindful awareness, children can tap into their creative potential and express themselves authentically.

One effective technique is mindful observation, where children observe their surroundings with a curious and open-minded attitude. This could involve observing the colors, shapes, and textures of objects in their environment or paying attention to the sounds and sensations around them. Through mindful observation, children learn to see the world with fresh eyes, uncovering inspiration in the ordinary moments of life.

Additionally, mindfulness practices such as visualization and guided imagery can help children access their inner creativity. By guiding them through vivid mental images and scenarios, these practices encourage children to tap into their imagination and explore new ideas and possibilities.

Overall, using mindfulness to explore creativity involves culti-vating a mindset of openness, curiosity, and non-judgment. By embracing the present moment with mindful awareness, chil-dren can unlock their creative potential and express themselves authentically through various forms of artistic expression.

10.2 Art Therapy and Mindfulness for Self-Expression

Art therapy combines the therapeutic benefits of creative expression with mindfulness principles to promote healing and self-discovery. For children with sensory issues, art therapy provides a safe and non-verbal means of communication, allowing them to express themselves freely and explore their emotions and experiences.

In art therapy sessions, children are encouraged to engage in various art-making activities such as drawing, painting, sculpting, and collage. These activities provide a creative outlet for children to express their thoughts, feelings, and sensations in a tangible and concrete form.

Mindfulness is integrated into art therapy sessions through guided mindfulness exercises and prompts that encourage children to approach the creative process with awareness and acceptance. For example, children may begin each session with a mindful breathing exercise to center themselves and cultivate presence before engaging in art-making activities.

During the art-making process, children are encouraged to practice mindfulness by focusing their attention on the sensory experience of creating art. This could involve paying attention to the colors, textures, and movements of the materials, as well as the sensations of their own bodies as they work.

Art therapists may also incorporate mindfulness-based interventions such as body-awareness exercises, progressive muscle relaxation, and guided imagery to help children regulate their sensory experiences and manage stress and anxiety.

Through art therapy and mindfulness, children with sensory issues can develop greater self-awareness, emotional regulation, and coping skills. They learn to express themselves creatively, process difficult emotions, and cultivate a sense of empowerment and resilience.

10.3 Writing and Journaling as Mindful Practices

Writing and journaling offer children with sensory issues a powerful means of self-expression, reflection, and self-discovery. Through mindful writing practices, children can explore their thoughts, feelings, and experiences in a safe and non-judgmental space, fostering greater self-awareness and emotional regulation.

To incorporate writing and journaling into mindfulness practices, children can start by setting aside dedicated time each day for journaling. This could be done first thing in the morning or before bedtime, providing a quiet and reflective space for children to connect with themselves.

Encourage children to begin each journaling session with a brief mindfulness exercise to center themselves and cultivate presence. This could involve a few minutes of mindful breathing or body scan meditation to ground themselves in the present moment.

Next, invite children to write freely and without inhibition, allowing their thoughts and feelings to flow onto the page without judgment. Encourage them to explore a wide range of topics, from their daily experiences and emotions to their hopes, dreams, and aspirations.

Mindful writing practices may also involve specific prompts or guided exercises designed to deepen self-awareness and insight. For example, children may be asked to reflect on a particular emotion or challenge they are facing and explore it in writing, using mindfulness techniques to observe their thoughts and feelings with curiosity and acceptance.

Additionally, encourage children to engage in creative writing exercises such as storytelling, poetry, or fiction writing as a means of self-expression. Through creative writing, children can explore their imagination, experiment with language, and express themselves in new and meaningful ways.

As children continue to engage in mindful writing and journaling practices, they develop greater self-awareness, emotional resilience, and coping skills. They learn to navigate their inner world with compassion and curiosity, fostering a deeper connection with themselves and others.

In conclusion, mindfulness offers children with sensory issues a powerful framework for exploring their creativity and self-expression. Whether through art therapy, writing, or other mindful practices, children can cultivate greater self-awareness, emotional regulation, and resilience, empowering them to navigate life's challenges with grace and authenticity.

11

Mindfulness in Nature

Chapter 11 explores the profound relationship between mindfulness and nature, offering insights into how connecting with the natural world can be a powerful tool for soothing the senses, engaging in outdoor mindfulness activities, and embracing ecotherapy for sensory wellness.

11.1 Connecting with Nature to Soothe the Senses

Nature has a remarkable ability to soothe the senses and promote a sense of calm and well-being. The sights, sounds, smells, and textures of the natural world can have a deeply calming effect on the nervous system, helping to reduce stress and anxiety. To connect with nature mindfully and soothe the senses, individuals can engage in practices such as:

1. Nature Walks: Taking leisurely walks in natural settings such as parks, forests, or along the beach can provide an opportunity

to immerse oneself in the beauty of nature. As individuals walk mindfully, they can focus on their breath, the sensation of their feet touching the ground, and the sights and sounds around them. By bringing awareness to the present moment, nature walks can help individuals feel grounded and connected to the world around them.

2. Forest Bathing: Originating from Japan, forest bathing, or shinrin-yoku, involves immersing oneself in the atmosphere of the forest to promote relaxation and well-being. During a forest bathing session, participants engage their senses by observing the trees, listening to the sounds of nature, and breathing in the fresh air. This mindful practice has been shown to reduce stress levels, lower blood pressure, and boost mood.

3. Nature Meditation: Finding a quiet spot in nature to sit and meditate can be a powerful way to cultivate mindfulness and inner peace. As individuals close their eyes and focus on their breath, they can tune into the natural rhythms of the environment, letting go of distractions and finding stillness within. Nature meditation can enhance feelings of connection to the earth and foster a sense of reverence for the natural world.

11.2 Outdoor Mindfulness Activities

Engaging in outdoor mindfulness activities provides an opportunity to deepen one's connection with nature while cultivating mindfulness skills. These activities encourage individuals to engage their senses fully and bring awareness to their experience in the present moment. Some outdoor mindfulness activities include:

1. Nature Observation: Find a quiet spot in nature and take a few moments to observe your surroundings mindfully. Notice the colors, shapes, and textures of the plants and trees around you. Listen to the sounds of birds singing or leaves rustling in the wind. Feel the warmth of the sun on your skin or the coolness of the breeze. By immersing yourself in the sensory experience of nature, you can cultivate a sense of presence and appreciation for the beauty of the natural world.

2. Mindful Walking: Practice walking mindfully in nature by paying attention to each step you take. Notice the sensations of your feet touching the ground and the muscles in your legs as they move. Take in the sights and sounds around you as you walk, allowing yourself to fully experience the present moment without judgment or distraction. Mindful walking can help to calm the mind, reduce stress, and increase awareness of the body and environment.

3. Nature Art: Use natural materials found in the environment to create art mindfully. Collect leaves, rocks, flowers, or other items and arrange them in a creative way. Allow yourself to become fully immersed in the process of creating, paying attention to the colors, textures, and shapes of the materials. Nature art can be a fun and therapeutic way to express creativity while fostering a deeper connection with the natural world.

11.3 Ecotherapy and Mindfulness for Sensory Wellness

Ecotherapy, also known as nature therapy or green therapy, is a therapeutic approach that harnesses the healing power of nature to promote emotional and psychological well-being.

Incorporating mindfulness practices into ecotherapy sessions can enhance sensory wellness and support overall health and wellness. Some ways in which ecotherapy and mindfulness can be combined for sensory wellness include:

1. Nature-Based Mindfulness Activities: Ecotherapy sessions often involve engaging in mindfulness practices in natural settings such as parks, gardens, or wilderness areas. Participants may participate in guided meditations, mindful walking, or nature-based art activities designed to promote sensory awareness and relaxation.

2. Sensory Exploration: Ecotherapy encourages participants to engage their senses fully and explore the natural world with curiosity and openness. Through activities such as sensory walks, individuals can deepen their connection to nature by paying attention to the sights, sounds, smells, and textures of the environment. This sensory exploration can help to reduce stress, increase feelings of relaxation, and promote a sense of connection to the earth.

3. Nature-Based Rituals: Ecotherapy often incorporates nature-based rituals and ceremonies designed to honor the natural world and foster a sense of reverence for the earth. Participants may engage in practices such as planting trees, making offerings to the land, or participating in seasonal celebrations to cultivate a deeper connection with nature and promote sensory wellness.

In conclusion, Chapter 11 explores the ways in which mindfulness can be integrated into our relationship with nature to soothe the senses, engage in outdoor mindfulness activities, and embrace ecotherapy for sensory wellness. By connecting with the natural world mindfully, individuals can cultivate a deeper sense of presence, connection, and well-being in their lives.

12

Mindfulness for Parents and Caregivers

Parenting a child with sensory issues can be both rewarding and challenging. It requires a significant amount of patience, understanding, and resilience. Parents and caregivers can integrate mindfulness into their lives to better support themselves and their children. This chapter focuses on three key aspects: practicing self-care, utilizing mindfulness techniques to manage parenting stress, and fostering mindful connections with their children.

12.1 Practicing Self-Care as a Caregiver

As a caregiver, it's easy to prioritize the needs of your child above your own. However, neglecting your own well-being can lead to burnout and decreased effectiveness in supporting your child. Practicing self-care is essential for maintaining your physical, mental, and emotional health.

Self-care can take many forms, and it's important to find what works best for you. This may include setting aside time each day for activities you enjoy, such as reading, exercising, or practicing a hobby. Additionally, self-care involves prioritizing healthy habits, such as getting enough sleep, eating nutritious meals, and staying hydrated.

Mindfulness plays a crucial role in self-care by helping caregivers stay present and attuned to their own needs. Mindful self-care practices can include mindfulness meditation, where caregivers take a few minutes each day to sit quietly and focus on their breath or bodily sensations. This can help calm the mind, reduce stress, and promote a sense of well-being.

Another aspect of self-care is setting boundaries and asking for help when needed. Caregivers should not hesitate to seek support from friends, family members, or professional resources. Building a support network can provide emotional validation, practical assistance, and much-needed respite.

12.2 Mindfulness Techniques for Parenting Stress

Parenting stress is a common experience for caregivers of children with sensory issues. The constant challenges and unpredictability of managing their child's needs can lead to feelings of overwhelm and exhaustion. Mindfulness techniques offer valuable tools for coping with parenting stress and cultivating resilience.

One effective mindfulness technique for managing stress is mindful breathing. Caregivers can practice this technique by taking slow, deep breaths and focusing their attention on the sensations of each inhale and exhale. This simple practice can help calm the nervous system, reduce tension, and bring a sense of clarity to the mind.

Mindful awareness of thoughts and emotions is another helpful technique for managing parenting stress. Caregivers can practice observing their thoughts and feelings without judgment, allowing them to acknowledge and accept whatever arises in the present moment. This practice can help caregivers develop a greater sense of self-awareness and emotional regulation.

In addition to formal mindfulness practices, caregivers can incorporate mindfulness into their daily activities. This can be as simple as practicing mindfulness while engaging in routine tasks, such as washing dishes or taking a walk. By bringing awareness to the present moment, caregivers can cultivate a greater sense of peace and presence in their daily lives.

12.3 Building Mindful Connections with Your Child

Building a strong and supportive relationship with your child is essential for their overall well-being. Mindfulness can help caregivers foster mindful connections with their children by promoting empathy, communication, and understanding.

One way to build mindful connections with your child is through mindful listening. Caregivers can practice attentive listening by giving their full attention to their child without interrupting or rushing to provide solutions. This allows children to feel heard and valued, strengthening the bond between caregiver and child.

Mindful communication is another important aspect of building mindful connections. Caregivers can practice speaking with kindness, honesty, and openness, fostering trust and mutual respect in the parent-child relationship. Mindful communication also involves being present and fully engaged during interactions with your child, rather than being distracted or preoccupied.

In addition to mindful listening and communication, caregivers can cultivate mindfulness in everyday interactions with their child. This can involve being fully present during shared activities, such as playing games or reading together, and savoring the moments of joy and connection that arise.

By practicing self-care, utilizing mindfulness techniques for managing stress, and building mindful connections with their children, caregivers can cultivate greater resilience, compassion, and well-being for themselves and their families.

13

Overcoming Challenges and Obstacles

Overcoming Challenges and Obstacles

Different challenges and obstacles may arise when incorporating mindfulness practices into the lives of children with sensory issues. This chapter provides a comprehensive guide on how to address resistance to mindfulness practices, troubleshoot common challenges, and seek support and resources to ensure successful implementation.

13.1 Addressing Resistance to Mindfulness Practices

Resistance to mindfulness practices can stem from various factors such as discomfort with the unfamiliar, skepticism about the effectiveness of mindfulness, or difficulty in maintaining focus and attention. Addressing resistance requires patience, understanding, and the implementation of strategies tailored to the individual needs of the child.

One approach is to start small and gradually introduce mindfulness practices in a non-threatening manner. Begin with short, simple exercises such as mindful breathing or sensory-focused activities that align with the child's interests and preferences. Providing choices and allowing the child to select activities they find enjoyable can increase engagement and reduce resistance.

It's essential to communicate the benefits of mindfulness in language that resonates with the child. Emphasize how mindfulness can help them feel calmer, more focused, and better equipped to manage sensory challenges. Encourage open dialogue and validate any concerns or hesitations the child may have, reassuring them that mindfulness is a skill that can be developed over time.

Modeling mindfulness practices can also be effective in overcoming resistance. Children are often influenced by the behavior of adults and caregivers, so demonstrating mindfulness techniques in a consistent and genuine manner can inspire curiosity and willingness to participate. Incorporate mindfulness into daily routines and activities, making it a natural part of the child's environment.

If resistance persists, it may be helpful to explore alternative approaches to mindfulness that better suit the child's preferences and needs. This could involve incorporating movement-based mindfulness practices such as yoga or tai chi, exploring creative outlets like art therapy, or engaging in nature-based mindfulness activities. Flexibility and adaptability are key in finding the right approach for each individual child.

13.2 Troubleshooting Common Mindfulness Challenges

Despite the benefits of mindfulness, children with sensory issues may encounter various challenges when practicing mindfulness. Common obstacles include difficulty in maintaining focus, heightened sensitivity to sensory stimuli, and resistance to certain mindfulness techniques. Troubleshooting these challenges requires a tailored approach that addresses the specific needs and preferences of the child.

One common challenge is maintaining focus during mindfulness practices, particularly for children with sensory processing difficulties. To overcome this, provide sensory supports such as weighted blankets, fidget toys, or soothing music to help regulate arousal levels and enhance concentration. Break mindfulness activities into shorter sessions and gradually increase the duration as the child's tolerance improves.

Another challenge is managing sensory overload during mindfulness practices, which can be overwhelming for children with sensory sensitivities. Create a calm and safe environment free from distractions, and encourage the use of grounding techniques such as deep breathing or focusing on specific sensory experiences to anchor attention. Offer choices and flexibility in mindfulness activities, allowing the child to adjust the intensity or duration based on their comfort level.

Resistance to specific mindfulness techniques is also common, especially if they involve unfamiliar sensations or movements. If a particular technique triggers discomfort or distress, explore alternative approaches that better align with the child's preferences. Provide options for customization and encourage experimentation to find what works best for the child.

It's important to acknowledge and validate any frustrations or setbacks encountered during mindfulness practices. Celebrate small successes and offer encouragement and support to motivate continued effort. Emphasize the process of learning and growth rather than focusing solely on outcomes, fostering a positive and resilient mindset.

13.3 Seeking Support and Resources

When facing challenges with mindfulness practices, it's essential to seek support and access available resources to ensure ongoing progress and success. There are various avenues for obtaining assistance, including professional guidance, peer support, and online resources.

Consulting with a qualified mental health professional or occupational therapist can provide valuable insights and personalized strategies for addressing specific challenges related to mindfulness and sensory issues. They can conduct assessments, develop tailored intervention plans, and offer ongoing support and guidance to both the child and their caregivers.

Peer support networks and community groups can also be valuable sources of encouragement and practical advice for navigating challenges with mindfulness practices. Connecting with other parents and caregivers who share similar experiences can provide a sense of solidarity and validation, as well as opportunities to exchange tips and strategies for overcoming obstacles.

In addition to seeking direct support, accessing online resources and educational materials can offer a wealth of information and guidance on mindfulness practices for children with sensory issues. Websites, blogs, and social media platforms dedicated to mindfulness, sensory processing disorders, and special needs parenting often provide practical tips, instructional videos, and printable resources that can be helpful in implementing mindfulness activities at home or in educational settings.

Furthermore, attending workshops, training sessions, or seminars on mindfulness and sensory integration can enhance knowledge and skills in effectively supporting children with sensory issues. These opportunities may be offered by local community centers, schools, or professional organizations specializing in child development and mental health.

By proactively seeking support and resources, caregivers and educators can gain the tools and knowledge needed to navigate challenges and promote the successful implementation of mindfulness practices for children with sensory issues. Collaboration with professionals, peer support networks, and access to relevant information can empower individuals to effectively address obstacles and foster positive outcomes in the journey toward mindfulness and sensory wellness.

14

Cultivating Mindful Communities

This chapter explores various aspects of creating supportive environments, integrating mindfulness into schools and communities, and fostering connections among families navigating similar experiences.

14.1 Creating Supportive Environments for Mindfulness

Supportive environments play a crucial role in facilitating mindfulness practices for children with sensory issues. To create such environments, educators, caregivers, and community leaders must prioritize understanding and accommodating the unique needs of these children. This involves:

1. Education and Awareness: Educating stakeholders about sensory processing disorders and the benefits of mindfulness is essential. Workshops, seminars, and informational sessions can raise awareness and promote understanding among teachers,

parents, and community members.

2. Accessible Resources: Providing accessible resources such as sensory-friendly spaces, mindfulness tools, and instructional materials ensures that children with sensory issues can fully participate in mindfulness activities. This may include sensory-friendly cushions, noise-canceling headphones, and visual aids to support their engagement.

3. Flexibility and Adaptability: Flexibility is key in accommodating children with sensory challenges. Mindfulness sessions should be adaptable to meet the diverse needs of participants. This may involve offering alternative activities, modifying sensory stimuli, or adjusting the duration and intensity of practices to ensure inclusivity.

4. Collaboration and Support: Collaborating with occupational therapists, mental health professionals, and other experts can enhance the effectiveness of mindfulness programs. By working together, communities can develop comprehensive strategies to support children with sensory issues and address their specific needs.

14.2 Mindfulness in Schools and Communities

Integrating mindfulness into schools and communities provides valuable opportunities for children with sensory issues to develop self-regulation skills and foster a sense of belonging. The following steps can help facilitate the integration of mindfulness practices:

1. Curriculum Integration: Incorporating mindfulness into the school curriculum allows students to practice mindfulness regularly. Integrating mindfulness into subjects like physical education, health education, and social-emotional learning promotes holistic development and enhances overall well-being.

2. Mindful Practices: Implementing daily mindfulness practices, such as mindful breathing exercises, body scans, and guided imagery, can help students cultivate awareness and reduce stress. These practices can be integrated into morning routines, classroom transitions, and designated mindfulness breaks throughout the day.

3. Teacher Training and Support: Providing professional development opportunities and ongoing support for teachers is essential for successful implementation. Training sessions on mindfulness techniques, classroom management strategies, and trauma-informed practices empower educators to create safe and supportive learning environments.

4. Parent and Community Engagement: Involving parents and community members in mindfulness initiatives fosters collaboration and strengthens the support network for children with sensory issues. Family mindfulness workshops, community events, and outreach programs encourage participation and promote mindfulness beyond the school setting.

14.3 Building Connections with Other Families

Building connections with other families facing similar challenges can provide invaluable support and resources. Creating opportunities for families to connect and share experiences fosters a sense of community and solidarity. Here are some ways to facilitate connections among families:

1. Support Groups: Establishing support groups for families of children with sensory issues allows parents to connect, share information, and provide mutual support. These groups can meet in person or online and provide a safe space for discussing challenges, sharing strategies, and celebrating successes.

2. Parent Education Workshops: Hosting workshops on topics related to sensory processing disorders, mindfulness, and self-care empowers parents with knowledge and resources. Workshops can feature guest speakers, interactive discussions, and hands-on activities to engage participants and build community.

3. Social Events: Organizing social events and recreational activities for families encourages bonding and camaraderie. Picnics, outings, and playdates provide opportunities for children to socialize while parents connect and build relationships in a relaxed setting.

4. Online Communities: Creating online communities, such as forums, Facebook groups, and online support networks, enables families to connect virtually and access support anytime, anywhere. These platforms facilitate information sharing, peer support, and networking opportunities for families worldwide.

By creating supportive environments, integrating mindfulness into schools and communities, and fostering connections among families, mindful communities can empower children with sensory issues to thrive and reach their full potential. Together, we can create a more inclusive and compassionate world where every child feels seen, heard, and supported.

15

Sustaining Mindfulness Practices

In the journey of integrating mindfulness into the lives of children with sensory issues, Chapter 15 serves as a guiding light towards sustaining these invaluable practices over time. Mindfulness isn't merely a tool to be used temporarily but rather a lifelong habit that can profoundly impact one's well-being. This chapter explains the strategies and approaches necessary to ensure that mindfulness becomes an integral part of a child's life, extending beyond childhood into adulthood.

15.1 Making Mindfulness a Lifelong Habit

The foundation of sustaining mindfulness practices lies in making it a habitual part of daily life. Habit formation is a process that involves consistent repetition and reinforcement. For children with sensory issues, creating routines around mindfulness can provide stability and predictability, which are essential for their comfort and progress.

One effective strategy is to integrate mindfulness into existing daily routines. For example, practicing mindful breathing during transitions between activities or incorporating short mindfulness exercises into bedtime routines can help establish consistency. Additionally, parents and caregivers can model mindfulness behaviors themselves, demonstrating its importance and making it a natural part of family life.

Consistency is key to habit formation, so setting realistic and achievable goals is crucial. Start with small, manageable steps and gradually increase the duration and complexity of mindfulness practices over time. Celebrate successes along the way to reinforce the habit and motivate continued practice.

Mindfulness can also be woven into various aspects of life, beyond formal meditation sessions. Encouraging mindful eating by paying attention to the sensory experience of food or incorporating mindfulness into leisure activities like art or nature walks helps reinforce its importance and relevance in everyday life.

15.2 Mindfulness Beyond Childhood: Adapting Practices

As children with sensory issues grow and mature, their needs and abilities evolve, requiring adaptations to their mindfulness practices. Adapting mindfulness techniques to meet these changing needs ensures that they remain relevant and beneficial throughout different stages of life.

Adolescence, in particular, presents unique challenges and opportunities for mindfulness practice. Teenagers may face increased stress and pressure from academic, social, and personal responsibilities, making mindfulness an invaluable tool for managing these challenges. Tailoring mindfulness practices to resonate with teenagers' interests and preferences can enhance their engagement and effectiveness.

Adapting mindfulness practices also involves recognizing individual differences and preferences. Not all techniques will resonate with every child, so it's essential to be flexible and open to exploring different approaches. Providing options and allowing children to choose the practices that resonate with them fosters a sense of autonomy and ownership over their mindfulness journey.

Furthermore, integrating mindfulness into broader life skills training can enhance its effectiveness and relevance. Teaching mindfulness alongside skills like emotional regulation, communication, and decision-making equips children with a holistic toolkit for navigating life's challenges.

15.3 Celebrating Progress and Growth

Acknowledging and celebrating progress is vital for sustaining mindfulness practices and fostering motivation and resilience. Celebrations serve as milestones that mark achievements and reinforce the value of mindfulness in one's life.

Recognizing progress can take many forms, from verbal praise and encouragement to tangible rewards or incentives. However, it's essential to focus on intrinsic motivation rather than external rewards to cultivate a genuine appreciation for mindfulness.

Celebrating progress also involves reflecting on the journey and recognizing the growth and development that has occurred. Encouraging children to reflect on how mindfulness has impacted their lives, from improved self-awareness to enhanced emotional regulation, reinforces its value and fosters a sense of pride and accomplishment.

Moreover, celebrations can be communal events that bring together family, friends, and mentors to share in the joy of achievement. Creating a supportive community around mindfulness reinforces its importance and provides encouragement and motivation during challenging times.

In conclusion, sustaining mindfulness practices requires a multifaceted approach that encompasses habit formation, adaptation to changing needs, and celebrating progress and growth. By embedding mindfulness into daily routines, adapting practices to meet evolving needs, and recognizing and celebrating achievements, children with sensory issues can cultivate a lifelong habit that enhances their well-being and resilience.

16

Conclusion

The conclusion of "Mindfulness for Kids with Sensory Issues" serves as a culmination of the journey embarked upon within the book, offering insights, reflections, and encouragement for both children and caregivers. Throughout the preceding chapters, we delved into the intricate relationship between mindfulness and sensory issues, exploring various practices, techniques, and strategies to foster greater well-being and resilience in children navigating these challenges. As we bring this journey to a close, it's essential to revisit the key themes and takeaways, reinforcing the transformative potential of mindfulness in the lives of children with sensory sensitivities.

First and foremost, we've underscored the importance of understanding sensory issues and their impact on daily life. From heightened sensitivity to certain stimuli to challenges in sensory processing, these experiences can significantly influence a child's emotions, behaviors, and overall quality of life. By gaining insight into the nuances of sensory issues, caregivers and educators can adopt a more empathetic and supportive approach, laying the groundwork for effective intervention and support.

Central to our exploration has been the introduction of mindfulness as a powerful tool for cultivating self-awareness, emotional regulation, and sensory integration. Mindfulness invites children to engage with their sensory experiences in a non-judgmental and compassionate manner, fostering a sense of calm and presence amidst the often overwhelming stimuli of the external world. Through practices such as mindful breathing, body scans, and sensory-focused activities, children learn to anchor themselves in the present moment, allowing them to navigate sensory challenges with greater ease and resilience.

Moreover, mindfulness has been shown to play a crucial role in promoting social and emotional development, an area of particular significance for children with sensory issues. By honing skills such as mindful listening, communication, and empathy, children can foster deeper connections with others, navigating social interactions with greater confidence and understanding. Additionally, mindfulness offers valuable support in managing emotions such as anger, anxiety, and frustration, empowering children to respond to challenging situations with clarity and composure.

Importantly, the benefits of mindfulness extend beyond individual well-being to encompass the broader context of family, school, and community support. Caregivers and educators play a pivotal role in nurturing mindfulness in children, modeling mindful behaviors and creating supportive environments for practice and reflection. By integrating mindfulness into daily routines, educational curricula, and therapeutic interventions, we can create a culture of mindfulness that permeates every aspect of a child's life, fostering holistic growth and resilience.

As we reflect on the journey of mindfulness for kids with sensory issues, it's essential to acknowledge the inherent challenges and obstacles along the way. Resistance to mindfulness practices, logistical constraints, and the complexities of sensory issues themselves may pose barriers to implementation and sustainability. However, by approaching these challenges with patience, flexibility, and creativity, we can overcome them together, drawing upon the collective wisdom and support of our communities.

Looking ahead, sustaining mindfulness practices beyond the pages of this book requires a commitment to ongoing learning, adaptation, and growth. Mindfulness is not a quick fix or a one-size-fits-all solution but rather a lifelong journey of self-discovery and transformation. As children continue to develop and evolve, so too must our approach to mindfulness, embracing new opportunities for exploration and innovation along the way.

In closing, "Mindfulness for Kids with Sensory Issues" serves as a beacon of hope and possibility for children and families navigating the complexities of sensory sensitivities. Through the transformative power of mindfulness, we have embarked upon a journey of self-discovery, resilience, and compassion, forging a path towards greater well-being and fulfillment for all. As we embrace the principles and practices of mindfulness in our daily lives, may we cultivate a world where every child feels seen, heard, and supported on their journey towards wholeness and self-discovery.

www.ingramcontent.com/pod-product-compliance
Lightning Source LLC
Chambersburg PA
CBHW050827250726

48653CB00006B/2475